YOU & FITNESS & HEALTH

Kate Fraser and Judy Tatchell

Consultant editor:
Paul McNaught-Davis

Designed by Sue Mims

CONTENTS

2 What are fitness and health?
4 Why you need exercise
6 What happens when you exercise?
8 Building up your stamina
10 Jogging
12 How your muscles work
14 Getting into shape
16 What is suppleness?
18 Exercising for suppleness
20 How to stay fit
22 Risks and injuries
24 Eating for health
26 Food and your body
28 All about skin
30 Healthy hair
32 Healthy teeth
34 Taking care of your eyes
36 Caring for hands and feet
38 Looking after your back
40 Rest and relaxation
42 Smoking, alcohol and drugs
44 Growing up
46 Checking your fitness progress
48 Index

Edited by Cheryl Evans
Illustrated by Brenda Haw, Kuo Kang Chen, Chris Lyon and Adam Willis

What are fitness and health?

Being healthy means your body is in good working order. You feel ready for anything.

Fitness refers to how much you can actually do with your body. Fitness training will enable you to do more and make you stronger and more supple.

Keeping fit can be fun. For example, all the activities in the picture below will help you keep fit.

In this book you can read about how to look after your body to keep yourself really fit and healthy.

> You probably already enjoy doing things that help keep you fit.

Exercise

One of the most important needs of your body is exercise. You can read about what happens when you exercise on pages 4-7. Regular exercise helps your body in three ways. It affects how well your muscles work (strength), your ability to keep going (stamina) and how flexible your body is (suppleness).

Stamina

If you have a lot of stamina you can probably run a long way or climb a long flight of stairs without getting puffed.

When you exercise, your body uses energy to keep itself going. To improve your stamina, you have to train your body to become more efficient and use less energy for the same amount of work. You can read all about this on pages 8-11.

Strength

Your bones are connected by muscles which you use when you move around, exercise, lift things and so on. Strength is the amount of force a muscle, or a group of muscles, can produce.

Different sports and fitness activities strengthen some muscles more than others. You can read about how your muscles work and how to improve them on pages 12-15.

Suppleness

If you are supple, you find it easy to bend, stretch and twist into different positions. Being supple is an important part of fitness as it affects the way you move when you exercise and lowers the risk of hurting yourself.

Some people can be very strong with lots of stamina but very little suppleness. You can read about suppleness on pages 16-19.

Keeping healthy

As well as regular exercise, your body has other major needs which are described on this page.

Food

Your body needs food to help it grow and repair itself and to provide energy to keep you going. You can read about the different kinds of foods you need in order to stay healthy and how your body uses them on pages 24-27.

Body care

Keeping yourself clean is an important part of staying healthy. It prevents the growth and spread of germs. It also helps prevent such things as certain skin disorders and tooth decay. You can read about how different parts of your body work including your skin, hair, teeth and eyes and how to clean and care for them on pages 28-37.

Posture

Your posture, or how you hold yourself when you stand, sit and move, can affect your digestion and feelings of energy or tension. It can also help prevent backache. You can read about this on pages 38-39.

Sleep and relaxation

Sleep is vital to your system. It gives your body time to grow, repair and refresh itself. Relaxation is also an important part of keeping healthy. It gets rid of tension and allows your body to "unwind". You can read all about this on pages 40-41.

Avoiding dangerous habits

Some people deal with stress by drinking too much alcohol, smoking too many cigarettes or taking drugs. You can read about how these can damage your body on pages 42-43.

Growing up

As you grow up, your body goes through all kinds of changes. Being fit and healthy during this time can help you feel more confident. Pages 44-45 explain these changes and how to deal with them.

Why bother to keep fit and healthy?

Good health means much more than not being ill. Here are some other benefits of keeping fit and healthy.

Looking good

Fitness and health can improve the way you look. Your body firms up and the condition of your skin, hair and so on improve. Good posture always makes you look better.

Feeling good

Being fit and healthy can give you more energy and can improve your self-confidence. Regular exercise helps to relax you and relieve tension. Looking after your body can make it stronger and more resistant to infectious diseases such as colds and flu.

A good level of fitness and health can lower the risk of illnesses, such as heart disease, arthritis and cancer, developing in later life.

Why you need exercise

Regular exercise keeps you fit and helps your body work more efficiently. It makes the different parts of your body strong and flexible. It keeps your whole system used to working hard which helps you maintain a good level of stamina. Below you can read about what happens to different parts of your body when you exercise.

Muscles

If you are laid up in bed for a long time your muscles shrink because you do not use them. This is why you feel weak after a long illness.

Your muscles need regular exercise to keep them firm and strong. If you do not use them enough they can become flabby and weak. This may put a strain on your joints as they do not get enough support.

Heart

Your heart works all the time pumping blood carrying oxygen around your body. When you exercise, your muscles need more oxygen than when you are less active. Your heart has to work harder. Exercise keeps your heart strong.

Lungs

I need more exercise. . . gasp!

Exercise makes you breathe more deeply and keeps the muscles in your chest strong. It also keeps your lungs used to taking in large amounts of air. This means that you are less likely to get out of breath when you exert yourself than someone who takes no exercise.

Energy, food and fat

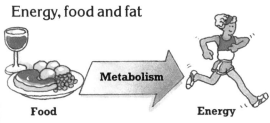

Metabolism

Food   Energy

Energy comes from the food you eat. If you eat more than you use for energy, the excess may be stored as fat. Exercise uses up energy and so can help you burn off fat.

The process of converting food to energy inside your body is called metabolism. The speed at which this happens is called your metabolic rate.

Energy and exercise

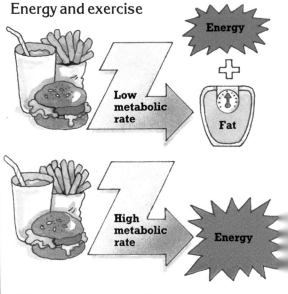

Energy

Low metabolic rate

Fat

High metabolic rate

Energy

Different people have different metabolic rates. A high rate can provide you with a lot of energy from your food. A lower rate produces energy more slowly and you tend to store more food as fat on your body. (There is more about this on page 26.)

Regular exercise can increase your metabolic rate. A higher metabolic rate releases more energy for you to use than a slow, sluggish one. This can make you feel more energetic in your daily life.

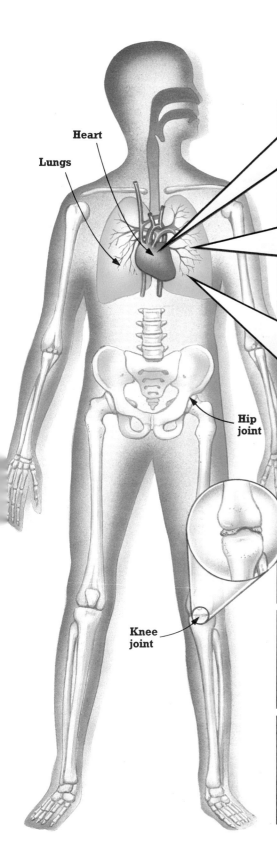

Heart

Lungs

Hip
joint

Knee
joint

Keeping healthy

Exercise can make you less vulnerable to certain illnesses and other problems, such as those shown below.

Heart disease

Strengthening your heart can improve your resistance to heart disease. This is the most common cause of death nowadays in the Western world.

Coughs

One of your body's ways of dealing with chest infections is to cough up the mucus, or phlegm, in your lungs. Strong chest and diaphragm muscles make coughing more effective.

Chest infections

If you have a chest infection, your lungs get blocked up and take in less air. This means that your blood absorbs less oxygen from the lungs. Your heart has to pump the blood through your body more quickly to supply it with oxygen. This puts more of a strain on a weak heart than on a strong heart.

Stiff joints

Without regular movement, joints may lose their suppleness. Certain sorts of exercise keep your joints flexible and strong. Straining your body by exercising too vigorously (over-exercising) can damage your joints, though, which may cause pain later in life.

Colds and flu

A healthy heart can help you resist diseases such as colds, flu and other infections. This is because a strong heart helps to keep your whole system healthy.

Feeling the cold

A strong heart can pump blood round your body efficiently. This helps to regulate your body temperature. People with poor blood circulation tend to get cold hands and feet very easily.

5

What happens when you exercise?

In order to work, your muscles need oxygen. The harder they work, the more they need. This page shows how oxygen in the air you breathe gets to your muscles via your lungs and blood system.

Exercise makes you work harder. It strengthens the heart muscles which pump blood round your body. It strengthens your chest muscles and increases the amount of air your lungs can hold.

How your lungs work

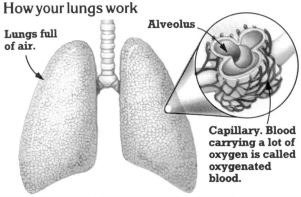

Alveolus

Lungs full of air.

Capillary. Blood carrying a lot of oxygen is called oxygenated blood.

Your lungs are made up of thousands of tiny air pockets called alveoli. These are covered with small blood vessels called capillaries.

When you breathe in, your alveoli fill with air. Oxygen from the air is absorbed into your blood through the capillaries. The oxygenated blood travels through a series of tubes to your heart.

How your heart works

Your heart works night and day pumping blood around your body. The blood travels through a network of tubes, called arteries, to all the different parts of your body. It travels back to your heart through veins.

When you exercise, your muscles need more oxygen, so your heart beats faster to pump more oxygenated blood to them. Your heart itself is a muscle, so it needs more oxygen to do this extra work. You breathe more often and more deeply to take in the extra oxygen.

Main vein carrying blood back to heart.

Main artery (aorta) taking blood from heart.

Pulmonary artery taking blood to lungs.

Pulmonary vein carrying oxygenated blood from lungs.

Blood carrying oxygen.

Blood without oxygen.

How energy is produced

Energy is produced in your muscles by chemical reactions between food you have eaten and chemicals in your body.*

A by-product of these chemical reactions, which your body does not need, is carbon dioxide. This is absorbed from your muscles back into the blood.

Your blood then carries it through veins to your heart.

Your heart pumps the blood containing carbon dioxide back to your lungs. Here, the carbon dioxide is absorbed into your lungs through the thin walls of the alveoli and you breathe it out.

*There is more about food and digestion on pages 26-27.

Exercise and heart disease

Heart disease develops over long periods when fatty deposits build up inside the arteries carrying blood to the heart muscle. This can starve the heart muscle of oxygen, causing it to stop beating. Lack of exercise, stress and eating a lot of fatty food* may all contribute to heart disease. Exercise gets blood moving swiftly through your arteries, so deposits are less likely to build up.

Exercise and high blood pressure

The force with which blood is squirted through your arteries is called blood pressure. Certain factors, such as stress, smoking, lack of exercise and being overweight can cause your blood vessels to deteriorate. Your blood pressure then goes up because your heart has to pump the blood faster through the vessels in order to carry the same amount to the muscles.

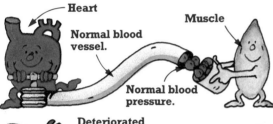

Heart

Muscle

Normal blood vessel.

Normal blood pressure.

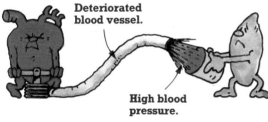

Deteriorated blood vessel.

High blood pressure.

High blood pressure is dangerous because it puts a strain on the heart and on the walls of the blood vessels.

Exercise can help since it encourages the blood vessels to open up and grow. Stress and tension may cause blood vessels to deteriorate. Exercise helps you to relax.

*There is more about fat on page 25.

Taking your pulse

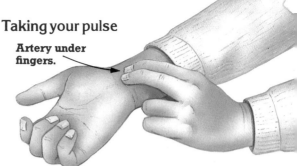

Artery under fingers.

You can take your pulse, or measure how fast your heart is beating, by pressing the artery on the inside of your wrist. Count how many beats you can feel in ten seconds and multiply by six. Everybody has a different pulse rate but an average adult rate at rest is about 70 beats per minute.

Exercise and your pulse rate

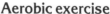
INCREASED PULSE RATE

Your pulse rate goes up when you exercise because your heart beats faster. You can check this yourself in the following way. Measure your pulse, then do something strenuous such as running upstairs. Then take your pulse again. As you become fitter your heart gets stronger and can squirt out more blood with each beat. It needs to beat less often, so your pulse rates at rest and during exercise become lower.

Aerobic exercise

Your heart, lungs and blood system together are called your aerobic system. Prolonged, rhythmical exercise such as jogging, skipping or cycling strengthens your aerobic system. This type of exercise is called aerobic exercise. There is more about this over the page.

Building up your stamina

A good level of stamina increases your energy and enables you to keep going longer during exercise. To improve your stamina you need gradually to strengthen your heart and lungs (your aerobic system) by doing some form of aerobic exercise. You can find out how to test your progress on the opposite page.*

All the activities on this page are aerobic activities. They also help to firm and strengthen muscles.

What is an aerobic activity?

Aerobic activities are those which you can sustain for long periods at a steady, even pace. Your aerobic system grows stronger and more efficient as your body adjusts to the new rate at which you need energy. Many activities are good for your aerobic system, especially jogging, cycling, skipping, swimming and brisk walking.

Other activities which are good for developing your stamina include rowing, canoeing, dancing, windsurfing, cross-country skiing and sports such as volleyball, basketball, football, badminton and table tennis. On page 47 you can check how different activities affect your stamina.

Walking is a gentle form of aerobic exercise. Walk at a fairly brisk pace and wear strong, comfortable shoes.

Jogging is a form of slow running. You can read more about it over the page.

You can skip at home alone or with friends. All you need is a skipping rope and a back yard.

Cycling builds up your leg muscles as well as your stamina. Try to include hills in your route to make you work harder.

Swimming exercises all your muscles and is excellent for stamina, strength and suppleness.

Warming up and cooling down

Before you do any form of exercise you need to warm up your body. This gets extra blood flowing to your muscles. They will need more oxygen when you start exercising. Without it they may become damaged. You can warm up by stretching and relaxing your muscles and flexing your joints, especially the ones you are going to use. There are some warming up exercises over the page.

After exercise, allow your body to cool down gently. Do some bending and stretching and slow down your movements until you are still. Relax so that your heart can get used to beating more slowly. All this will help to prevent stiffness and soreness the next day.

*If you have heart trouble, diabetes, asthma, high blood pressure or any chronic condition, consult your doctor before you take up any fitness activity.

How to go about training

Aerobic exercise means making your heart work a bit harder for a long time. It is a gentle, sustained form of exercise. Your pulse rate should rise slightly during exercise. Short bursts of intense exercise that dramatically increase your pulse rate will not do much for your aerobic system. They exhaust you and you have to stop.

The chart below shows a target zone for your pulse rate during exercise. Take your pulse* before you start. Half way through your exercise, take it again. If it is below the target zone, increase what you do by a small amount each time you exercise. Swim another length or jog a bit further. Increase the distance you cover rather than your pace, so you do not overtire yourself. Take your pulse as soon as you finish exercising to see if it is within the target zone.

Pulse rate chart

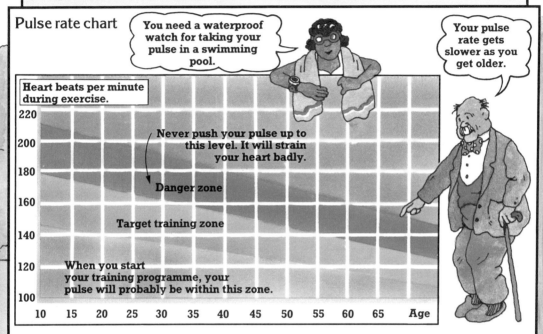

You need a waterproof watch for taking your pulse in a swimming pool.

Your pulse rate gets slower as you get older.

Heart beats per minute during exercise.

Never push your pulse up to this level. It will strain your heart badly.

Danger zone

Target training zone

When you start your training programme, your pulse will probably be within this zone.

220 200 180 160 140 120 100

10 15 20 25 30 35 40 45 50 55 60 65 Age

As your stamina increases, you will be able to do the same amount of exercise for less effort. You need to do more to keep your pulse rate in the target zone and for your progress to continue.

If your pulse goes into the danger zone while exercising, stop and let it fall. You are working too hard (over-exercising). This will not improve your stamina and it can be dangerous.

Basic equipment

When you are exercising you need to keep warm. You tire more easily when you are cold as your body has to use more energy trying to warm you up. The supply of blood to your muscles may be reduced, causing injury. Wear layers of clothing that you can peel off as you warm up.

★ Trainers are good for walking, cycling, jogging, skipping and many other sports.

★ Loose-fitting shorts and T-shirts allow you to move freely and do not rub. Cotton ones absorb sweat. Materials which do not absorb sweat, such as nylon, can be uncomfortable.

★ Track suits are useful for warming up and to put on after exercise, especially out of doors.

★ Cycling shorts have leather patches which prevent your thighs getting rubbed on the saddle.

*You can find out how to take your pulse on page 7.

Jogging

Jogging is a good way to improve your stamina. You do not need any special equipment other than loose clothing and strong training or running shoes. On these pages you can read about how to develop a good jogging style and there are some useful warming up exercises. There is also a training programme to help you keep track of your progress.

How to jog

When you jog, run at a slow, comfortable pace. If you get out of breath or your muscles hurt, slow down or stop to recover. Here you can see how to move and breathe when you jog.

★ Breathe regularly through your mouth.

★ Stay upright – do not lean too far forwards.

★ Keep elbows slightly bent but relaxed. Shake arms from time to time to relieve tension.

If you cannot talk while jogging, you are going too fast.

★ Let your heel strike the ground before your toe.

★ Do not lift your legs too high: try to glide rather than stamp.

Warming up exercises

Before you start jogging, warm up thoroughly. These exercises warm up the muscles you will be using. Repeat each one ten times.

Stand an arm's length from a wall with your hands flat against it. Bend arms to stretch back of legs.

Repeat the previous exercise with your legs bent. This stretches the sides of your calves.

Lie on the floor with your legs bent and palms on the floor. Sit up using your stomach muscles.

Sit with legs apart. Try to touch your toes, keeping your back straight.

Stand with feet together. Jump legs apart, then back together.

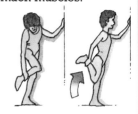

Grasp ankle. Pull until heel touches buttocks. Repeat with other foot.

Jogging for beginners

Start by walking briskly for about 20 minutes three or four times a week. Jog for a few minutes at intervals during your walk. Over the weeks, jog more and walk less until you can jog without stopping for 20 minutes.

You can use the chart below as a training programme but adjust it if you feel you are pushing yourself too hard. It shows how to combine jogging and walking. As you increase the amount of jogging, the total exercise time goes down at first until your body is used to the extra effort.

The numbers in the second column tell you how many times to exercise each week.

Minutes spent exercising.		1	2	3	4	5	6	7	8	9	10	11	12	13	14	15	16	17	18	19	20	21
Week 1	×3														▓				▓			
Week 2	×3							▓				▓				▓						
Week 3	×4			▓	▓			▓	▓			▓	▓									
Week 4	×4	▓	▓	▓		▓		▓	▓	▓		▓	▓	▓								
Week 5	×4																					
Week 6	×4																					

☐ Walk for 1 minute.   ▓ Jog for 1 minute.

Safety hints

Try to jog on softer ground, such as turf rather than concrete.

If you live in a town or city, try to jog early before the air gets filled with smoke and fumes.

If you jog at night, wear white or reflective clothing so that you can be seen.

Running shoes and trainers

Here are some hints on buying running shoes or trainers.

★ Short shoelaces are better than long ones which you might trip over.

★ There should be about 1cm (a third of an inch) between your toes and the end of the shoe. This gives your feet space to expand when they get hot.

★ Avoid plastic shoes. Your feet may get too hot.

★ Avoid shoes with heel tabs. They may rub against your ankles.

Heel tab

★ Get shoes with thick, cushioned soles to protect your feet.

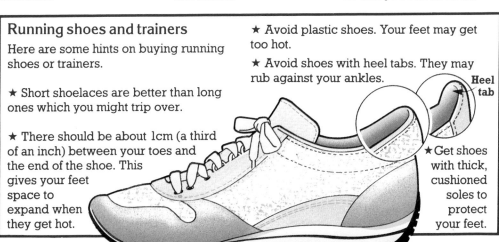

How your muscles work

You have over 600 muscles in your body. You use them to move, breathe and even to stand still. On these pages you can read about how muscles work and how to make them stronger.

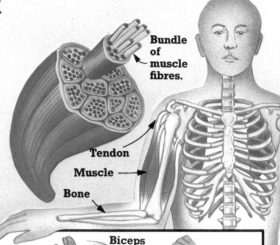

Bundle of muscle fibres.

Tendon

Muscle

Bone

What is a muscle made of?

The muscles you use to control your movements consist of bundles of long, thin cells called fibres. A muscle is attached to a bone at each end by a flexible cord or sheet called a tendon.

What happens when you move?

Relaxed fibres.

Contracted fibres.

Biceps
Triceps

The harder you exert a muscle, the more fibres you use and the more it will bulge out.

When your muscles are relaxed, the fibres are relatively soft. When you want to move, your brain sends signals to the fibres in the muscles you need to control.

The signals tell each fibre to shrink in length, or contract. The whole muscle becomes firmer, shorter and fatter. The bone it is attached to is forced to move.

Most muscles which you use to move are arranged in pairs. For example, the biceps contracts and the triceps relaxes to bend your arm. The opposite happens to straighten it.

Types of muscle fibre

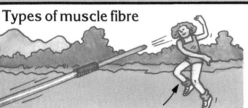

Athletes such as javelin throwers and sprinters need lots of fast twitch fibres to give them short bursts of strength.

You have two kinds of muscle fibre. The kind which provide immediate strength in short bursts are called fast twitch fibres. These contain a form of stored energy called ATP. This enables them to work without using oxygen, or anaerobically.

Slow twitch fibres use energy at a slower rate, so you use them for activities which require stamina. They work aerobically, that is by converting oxygen and nutrients in your blood to energy.

Building up muscle

To develop muscles, you need to make them work hard for a short time. The size of the fibres increases to cope with the extra work. For instance, you can build muscles in your arms and shoulders by doing press-ups. Other methods include swimming, rowing and training with weights in gymnasiums on specially designed equipment.* To build muscles, you normally need to work them harder than in aerobic exercise (see pages 8-9).

12

*You can read about ways to strengthen your muscles over the page.

How muscles affect your shape

If you do not exercise your muscles they become weaker and flabby. They may shrink in size. This affects the shape of your body.

Weak muscles

It is easy to confuse weak muscles with fat.

Weak stomach muscles cannot hold your internal organs in place, which gives you a pot belly. This pulls on the spine and may cause back problems. It also encourages bad posture which affects your appearance.

Strong stomach muscles pull the flesh and organs underneath into shape.

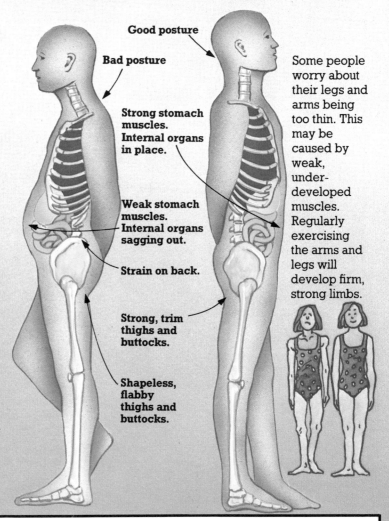

Good posture

Bad posture

Strong stomach muscles. Internal organs in place.

Weak stomach muscles. Internal organs sagging out.

Strain on back.

Strong, trim thighs and buttocks.

Shapeless, flabby thighs and buttocks.

Some people worry about their legs and arms being too thin. This may be caused by weak, under-developed muscles. Regularly exercising the arms and legs will develop firm, strong limbs.

Stiffness and cramp

When you come in from exercising . . .

don't just stop suddenly . . .

or the next morning . . .

you will be stiff.

When you exercise vigorously, your muscles produce a substance called lactic acid. If you over-exercise or stop exercising suddenly, it gets left behind with other waste products in your muscles. This can cause stiffness for a day or two. If you slow down gently, the lactic acid is more likely to be flushed away in your bloodstream.

A feeling of cramp is caused by prolonged contractions of one or more muscles. It may be due to a lack of nutrients and fluid in the muscle fibres but no one really knows.

Proper warming up, a good diet* and drinking plenty of fluid will help to avoid cramp. To relieve it, try gently stretching and massaging the painful muscle.

*See pages 24-25 for more about healthy diets.

Getting into shape

Here are some activities which are good for building muscles and improving your shape. There is also some advice about equipment and some simple exercises to help strengthen particular muscles.

Weight training

Weight training. This is different from weight lifting, where the aim is to lift the heaviest possible weight.

Weight lifting.

This machine has stacks of weights which you lift and lower using ropes and pulleys.

You can strengthen almost any muscle group in your body by doing different exercises with light weights. This is known as weight training. You do not need expensive equipment for this. You can use your body weight or books as the loads to lift, as shown in the exercises on the opposite page.

Many gymnasiums have special equipment for exercising different muscles. You can adjust the load on the machine according to how strong you are. This results in a controlled, efficient form of exercise. You should never do it without a supervisor present. Normally you have to pay to use the equipment.

Exercise to avoid

The following types of exercise may build big muscles but can be dangerous.

Isometric exercise

Some muscle-building methods and apparatus make muscles work as hard as possible against immovable objects. This is called isometric exercise. It can encourage high blood pressure and should be avoided.

Pressing your palms together as hard as possible is an isometric exercise, so avoid it.

Free weight training

Exercising with free weights (very heavy weights unattached to machines) can easily injure muscles.

Building up your strength

Here are some activities which are good for developing muscular strength. Others include swimming, wrestling, cycling, ice skating, soccer and tennis.

Cross-country skiing strengthens your whole body. It is easier for beginners than downhill skiing.

Canoeing can be exciting and strengthens your upper arms and back.

Riding depends on balance and develops your back, buttock and leg muscles.

Activities such as digging or scrubbing help develop strength. You may develop one arm more than the other, though.

Rowing strengthens your back and legs. They supply the power to pull the oar through the water.

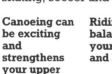

Muscle-toning exercises

The following exercises strengthen and tone different muscles. For the last two, you need to use a light weight. A few books in a bag will do. Start with one or two and increase the load as you get stronger. Make sure the loads are even and warm up properly before you start. Repeat each exercise 10-15 times.

Thighs

Keep knees, hips and shoulders in a straight line.

Kneel up straight. Lean back while raising your arms. Hold this position for four seconds. Straighten up again while lowering your arms.

Triceps

Start with this.

When stronger, try this.

Lie down with your palms on the floor by your shoulders. Push your body up until your arms are straight. Lower your body and repeat.

Buttocks

As you get better at this you will be able to raise your legs higher.

Lie face down, with your arms by your sides. Point your toes and raise your legs, keeping them straight. Hold for five seconds. Lower your legs gently.

Stomach

Sit upright on chair, with legs stretched out. Hold sides of chair and slowly draw legs towards chest, keeping back straight. Lower legs and repeat.

Biceps

Light weight

Sit in chair, holding weights or a light bag of books in each hand. Bend arms and lift bags towards shoulders. Lower slowly. Increase weight slowly over weeks.

Calves

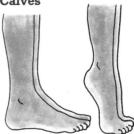

Stand with feet flat on the floor. Rise on to your toes. Lower yourself gently and repeat. You can also do this holding a light bag of books or a weight in each hand.

Weight-training equipment

Here is some of the equipment used in weight training. You should learn to use it under supervision. Never use a weight heavier than you feel comfortable with or that makes your muscles hurt.

Dumbells are short rods fitted with weights at either end. They can be held in either hand.

Barbells are long rods to which different weights are fitted. You hold them with both hands at once.

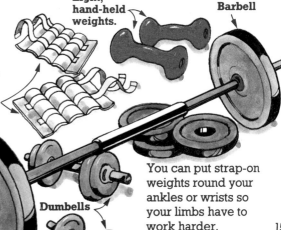

Light, hand-held weights.

Barbell

Strap-on weights

Dumbells

You can put strap-on weights round your ankles or wrists so your limbs have to work harder.

15

What is suppleness?

Being able to bend and stretch easily is called suppleness. It is just as important as strength and stamina. Lack of suppleness can restrict your range of movement and make you more prone to injury and stiffness.

Most people will never be as supple as trained dancers or top gymnasts but everyone can improve a little by exercising correctly.

How your joints work

How supple you are depends on how flexible your joints and muscles are. Different joints are shaped to allow different movements. The picture shows a ball and socket joint in the hip which allows movement in all directions. The thigh bone has a ball-shaped piece at the end which fits into a socket in the pelvis.

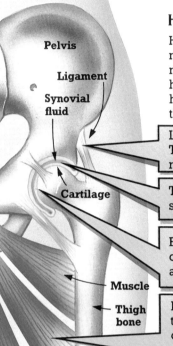

Pelvis

Ligament

Synovial fluid

Cartilage

Muscle

Thigh bone

Ligaments are tough, stringy cords between the bones. They support the joint and limit its movement so that it does not bend too far and get damaged.

The joint is lubricated by a substance called synovial fluid so that the bones do not grate on each other.

Each end of the bone is covered with a rubbery cushion called cartilage. This protects it when you move and absorbs the shock when you knock a joint.

Muscles help to support your joints. The stronger they are, the stronger your joints will be. They pull on tendons connected to your bones to move joints. (See page 12 for more about how muscles work.)

What makes you supple?

The stretchier your muscles and tendons, the more supple you are.

Ligaments do not stretch much but some people have longer, looser ligaments than others. People with so-called double joints have very loose ligaments. This can be a disadvantage as the joint may not be supported.

Regular stretching exercises stretch the tissue surrounding the muscle fibres so the muscles can lengthen. The exercises keep your joints supplied with blood and used to a wide range of movement.

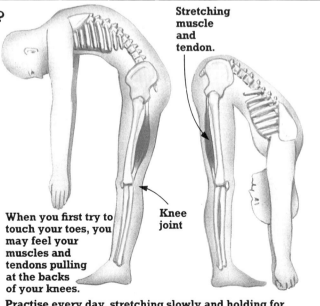

Stretching muscle and tendon.

When you first try to touch your toes, you may feel your muscles and tendons pulling at the backs of your knees.

Knee joint

Practise every day, stretching slowly and holding for about six seconds. Soon you will be able to bend further.

Risks to your joints

If you do not keep supple, the muscles round your joints eventually tighten up. This may cause a feeling of stiffness when you stretch and it puts pressure on your joints when you exercise.

If you force a joint beyond its natural range of movement, you may tear, or sprain, a ligament. You may also over-stretch, or strain, a muscle. If you stretch a ligament over a certain limit, it may not fully tighten up again. This leaves the joint with less support.

When you sprain your ankle, you tear one of the ligaments supporting your foot.

Sprained ankle. →

Torn ligament.

Certain activities such as jogging and cycling consist of the same movement repeated lots of times. Your muscles get used to working in the same direction and stretching the same distance. As they grow stronger, they get shorter. This restricts your suppleness. Exercises such as those over the page help to prevent this.

You can avoid most injuries if you warm up properly and do not over-exercise. Being overweight, carrying uneven loads and bad posture put strain on muscles and joints.

Unbalanced loads put uneven pressure on muscles and joints.

Why keep supple?

Here are some reasons for keeping supple. Remember never to force your body beyond what feels comfortable.

★ Suppleness helps to prevent sprains and long-term damage. It also reduces stiffness in muscles after exercise.

★ Keeping supple teaches you your body's limits. This lowers the risk of over-exercising and improves your co-ordination.

★ Supple joints encourage good posture. Stiff joints can restrict it.

★ Keeping supple can help make your movements smooth and confident rather than stiff and awkward.

★ Bending and stretching help to relax you and reduce stress.

You need to be very supple before you can stretch like this.

Exercising for suppleness

Slow, gentle stretching is the best way to loosen your muscles and develop suppleness. Fast, vigorous movements may cause strain and damage. Some people are much more supple than others and you should not stretch yourself beyond what feels comfortable.

If you do the exercises on these pages regularly you will gradually find you can stretch further.

How supple are your shoulders?

Hold a ruler and note where your index finger is. Push the ruler over your shoulder and grip it as far up as possible with the other hand. Let go with the first hand. Note where your other index finger is.

Work out the distance between the first reading and the second. This is the distance between your hands behind your back. The more supple you are the smaller the distance is.

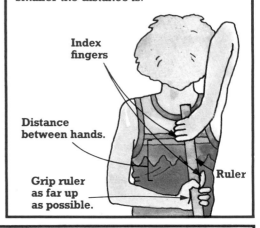

Index fingers

Distance between hands.

Grip ruler as far up as possible.

Ruler

Suppleness exercises

Below are some suppleness exercises. You can include them as part of your normal warming up routine.*
Repeat the top three exercises ten times in each direction and the last three exercises five times each.

Any gentle bending and stretching is good for keeping supple.

Head rolling

Gently roll head forwards, sideways, backwards and round to the front again.

Shoulder circles

Shrug shoulders. Circle them smoothly back, down, forwards and up.

Hip circles

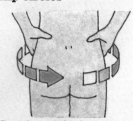

Stand upright, hands on hips. Swing hips round in large circles.

Back stretch

Sit clasping feet in front of you. Lean forehead down towards feet. Hold for five seconds. Relax.

Leg stretch

Lie down. Clasp one knee and pull gently towards chest keeping other leg straight and flat on the floor. Repeat other side.

Body stretch

Stretch up as high as you can. Then bend down keeping legs straight and try to touch toes.

The warming up exercises on page 10 are also suppleness exercises.

Yoga

The ancient philosophy of yoga includes forms of exercise which stretch and relax your body in different postures. It is gentle, non-competitive and can be very relaxing. Below are some beginners' yoga exercises. When you do them, breathe normally and be careful not to over-strain yourself. To learn more about yoga, try to find a proper yoga class.

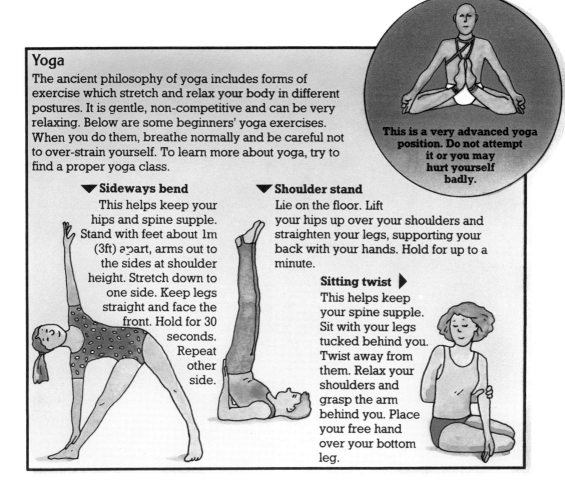

This is a very advanced yoga position. Do not attempt it or you may hurt yourself badly.

▼ Sideways bend

This helps keep your hips and spine supple. Stand with feet about 1m (3ft) apart, arms out to the sides at shoulder height. Stretch down to one side. Keep legs straight and face the front. Hold for 30 seconds. Repeat other side.

▼ Shoulder stand

Lie on the floor. Lift your hips up over your shoulders and straighten your legs, supporting your back with your hands. Hold for up to a minute.

Sitting twist ▶

This helps keep your spine supple. Sit with your legs tucked behind you. Twist away from them. Relax your shoulders and grasp the arm behind you. Place your free hand over your bottom leg.

Ways of keeping supple

Activities which will help you keep supple include swimming, volleyball, skiing, skating, dancing, gymnastics, judo and tennis.

Ballet is a demanding form of dancing. You need to go to proper ballet classes to learn how to do it.

Ice skating can be exhilarating, and is good for your circulation, balance and posture.

← In jazz, modern and disco dancing, you relax and move to the music. You need a good sense of rhythm.

In gymnastics you work on the floor and on apparatus such as the beam and asymmetric bars. You need supervision and careful coaching.

19

How to stay fit

In order to stay fit, you need to make exercise a regular part of your life. On these pages you can find out how you can do this and about how to develop a balanced training programme. Some people find it hard to stay fit because they get bored with exercising on their own. An enjoyable way to stay fit is to play sports and games with other people.

Team games

If you play team sports, such as soccer and baseball, you can have fun, see your friends and keep in trim at the same time. Many people find it easier to stick to a regular time for playing sports with friends than to exercise alone. Most games are good for stamina and strength and you get a sense of achievement as you improve.

Many team games do not need much equipment. You can easily play soccer using coats as goal posts.

Most sports centres have courts which you can hire for playing squash, basketball, volleyball, badminton and tennis.

Racket games

Games you play with a racket, such as tennis, squash and badminton, seem quite strenuous. However, you have to be quite good before you get much exercise on court. This is because you play in short bursts.* Here is a chart showing how much exercise you get in an average half hour's play. Minutes spent taking up your position, picking up balls and so on are marked by a net. The rest of the half hour is actual exercise time.

Squash					
Badminton					
Tennis					
5	10	15	20	25	30

Minutes

Athletics

You may be able to do athletics at school or with a local club. It is an exciting way to keep fit. If you want to win a race, to jump higher, or to throw further you have a real reason to train and exercise regularly. You will also be able to keep track of your progress.

You need strength for sprinting, shot putting, discus and javelin throwing.

You need to be strong and supple for the high jump.

You need stamina for middle-distance and long-distance running.

If you are very unfit, slowly build up the amount you play.

Balanced training

Sports affect your strength, stamina and suppleness in different ways. You can see this on the chart on page 47. The picture below shows the different categories of exercise you need to do to keep your whole body in good condition and to achieve a good balance of exercise.

You can use the Weekly Fitness Plan at the bottom of the page to help you sustain a good level of fitness.

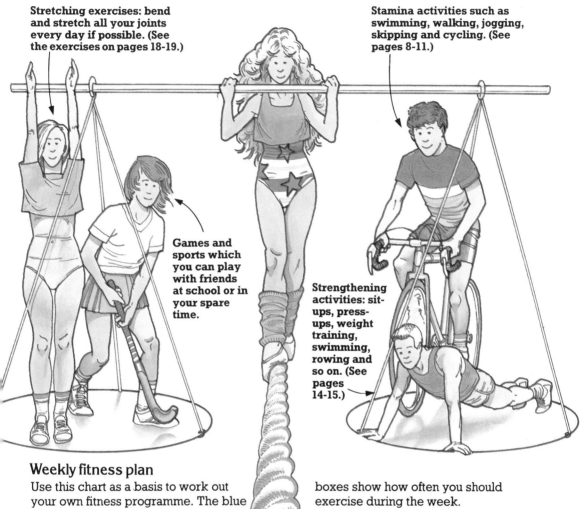

Stretching exercises: bend and stretch all your joints every day if possible. (See the exercises on pages 18-19.)

Stamina activities such as swimming, walking, jogging, skipping and cycling. (See pages 8-11.)

Games and sports which you can play with friends at school or in your spare time.

Strengthening activities: sit-ups, press-ups, weight training, swimming, rowing and so on. (See pages 14-15.)

Weekly fitness plan

Use this chart as a basis to work out your own fitness programme. The blue boxes show how often you should exercise during the week.

Time spent per session. ▶	10 minutes of stretching.	30 minutes building stamina.	30 minutes of strengthening.	1 hour playing games.
Day 1				
Day 2				
Day 3				
Day 4				
Day 5				
Day 6				
Day 7				

Risks and injuries

If you play sports or exercise regularly you may hurt yourself from time to time. Below you can read about some of the most common causes of injury and how you can reduce the risk of getting hurt.

Cause of injury

How to avoid it

Sudden muscular contraction
If one of your muscles contracts strongly and the opposite muscle does not stretch quickly enough it gets torn. For instance, you can damage your hamstring (back thigh muscle) when you contract your quadriceps (front thigh muscle) during sprinting.

Warm up your muscles thoroughly before you start exercising. Try to keep your body supple.

Lack of skill
If you are not very good at a sport you are more likely to hurt yourself. For instance, if you kick at a ball and miss, your kicking leg straightens with a lot of force, straining your knee. Also, your back thigh muscles may get over-stretched.

Keep your muscles supple. When playing ball games, watch the ball carefully to help you hit or kick it.

Tiredness
You are more likely to hurt yourself when you are starting to tire towards the end of a game or an exercise session.

You need a good level of stamina to keep you going throughout the game.

Over-exercising
If you over-exercise muscles, they pull on your tendons too hard and the connections may get broken. You need to be especially careful before the age of 15. Until then your joints are not fully developed.

Don't be too ambitious in what you ask your body to do. Warm up properly and increase the amount of exercise slowly.

Running on hard surfaces
You can damage your ankles, knees, hips and spine by too much running on hard ground.

Wear running shoes or strong trainers and run on soft surfaces where possible.

Knocks, cuts and bruises
You may get cut and bruised during games from falling or bumping into other people. You can hurt yourself quite badly by falling off a bike.

Wear protective clothing (pads for football, cycling gloves for cycling) and check all equipment for sharp edges. Try to play against people of a similar standard to you. Stick to the rules of the game.

How to treat injuries

Here you can read about how to deal with different injuries. If you are in a lot of pain, you should see a doctor.

Cuts and bruises

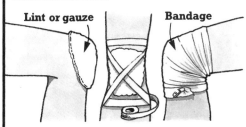

Lint or gauze   Bandage

Wash a cut under running water. Cover a large wound with gauze or lint (not cotton wool). Wrap a bandage round it firmly but not too tightly. If the cut is deep or dirty you should see a doctor for proper cleaning or stitches. If you have a bruise, avoid situations such as games where you might knock it.

Knocks on the head

If you knock yourself out or if you feel sick or dizzy after a bang on the head, see a doctor to check for any damage.

Sprains and strains

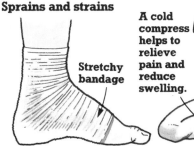

Stretchy bandage

A cold compress helps to relieve pain and reduce swelling.

Sprains cause the joint where the ligament is torn to swell up. Strains feel sore where you have over-stretched the muscle. Lie down and rest the joint on a cushion raised higher than your head. Put a cold compress, such as a cloth soaked in icy water, on the joint. Once you are able to move without too much pain, strap the joint with a stretchy bandage to support it.

See a doctor if it is very painful in case you have broken something.

Fractures and dislocations

Never move someone in great pain.

If someone is in great pain, they may have broken or dislocated a joint. Do not move them and get medical help immediately.

Food and exercise

Do not take vigorous exercise straight after a meal.

Never exercise immediately after eating. Much of your blood is being diverted to your stomach to help digest your food. If you start exercising, your muscles may not have enough blood and will not work efficiently. You may feel sick or faint.

Health risks and exercise

If you have certain conditions such as diabetes, asthma, heart trouble or high blood pressure, you should consult your doctor before taking up any fitness activity. For most of these conditions the right sort of exercise will do you good.

Many famous sportsmen and women, including marathon runners, are diabetic or have asthma.

23

Eating for health

What you eat affects your health. There is a lot of temptation from advertisements and shop displays to eat food which is bad for you. Here you can read about what you need to eat for a healthy diet and which foods you should avoid.

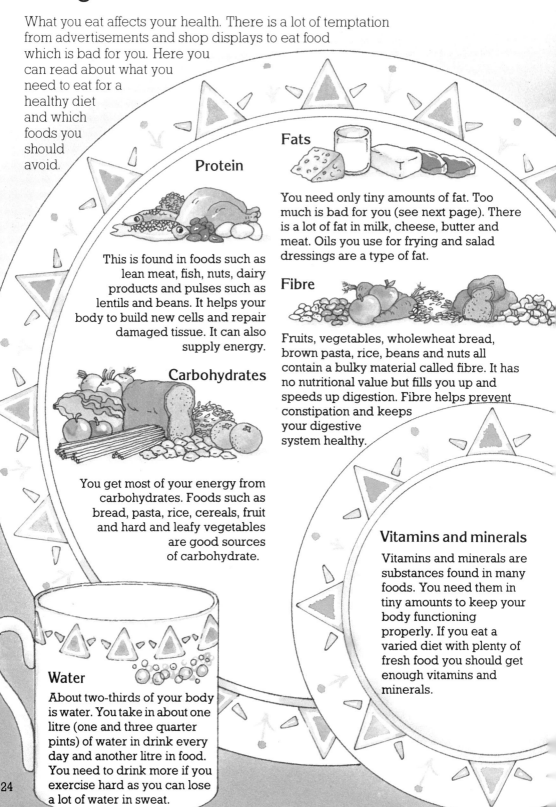

Protein

This is found in foods such as lean meat, fish, nuts, dairy products and pulses such as lentils and beans. It helps your body to build new cells and repair damaged tissue. It can also supply energy.

Carbohydrates

You get most of your energy from carbohydrates. Foods such as bread, pasta, rice, cereals, fruit and hard and leafy vegetables are good sources of carbohydrate.

Fats

You need only tiny amounts of fat. Too much is bad for you (see next page). There is a lot of fat in milk, cheese, butter and meat. Oils you use for frying and salad dressings are a type of fat.

Fibre

Fruits, vegetables, wholewheat bread, brown pasta, rice, beans and nuts all contain a bulky material called fibre. It has no nutritional value but fills you up and speeds up digestion. Fibre helps prevent constipation and keeps your digestive system healthy.

Vitamins and minerals

Vitamins and minerals are substances found in many foods. You need them in tiny amounts to keep your body functioning properly. If you eat a varied diet with plenty of fresh food you should get enough vitamins and minerals.

Water

About two-thirds of your body is water. You take in about one litre (one and three quarter pints) of water in drink every day and another litre in food. You need to drink more if you exercise hard as you can lose a lot of water in sweat.

Foods to avoid

Some things are bad for you if you eat a lot of them. Try to cut down on the things shown on this page.

Sugar

Cereals, Fizzy drinks, Mayonnaise, Tomato soup, Some frozen pizzas, Frozen peas, Corned beef

Sugar is a carbohydrate. It provides energy but contains no other nutrients. It rots teeth and can cause spots. It is very fattening and this may contribute to high blood pressure. You may eat more than you realize because it is in many packaged foods, such as those above.

Fat

Fats which come from animals such as fat in milk, butter, meat and eggs are called saturated fats. They contain a substance called cholesterol. Over long periods, this can cause fatty deposits in your arteries, leading to heart disease.

To prevent this, replace animal fats with vegetable fats, called polyunsaturated fats. Switch to polyunsaturated margarine instead of butter and use vegetable oils for cooking. Too much fat of any kind may make you overweight and put a strain on your heart.

Food additives

Much packaged food has substances added to it to brighten the colour, sharpen the flavour, or preserve it. Many additives are harmless but some people are allergic to certain types and may suffer sickness, faintness and skin rashes.

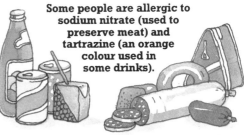

Some people are allergic to sodium nitrate (used to preserve meat) and tartrazine (an orange colour used in some drinks).

Salt

Too much salt may contribute to high blood pressure, circulatory problems and arthritis in some people. Once you get used to eating less salt you may find many packaged foods much too salty.

Coffee and tea

Caffeine only provides a temporary "lift".

Coffee and tea contain a drug called caffeine. This perks you up for about three hours but then you feel more tired than you were before. It can keep you awake at night and make you jumpy and tense if you drink too much.

Hints for a healthy diet

★ Eat as much fresh food as possible. Tinning and freezing food destroy some of its vitamins and minerals.
★ Cut down on saturated animal fat by drinking skimmed milk and eating low fat cheese and white meat and fish rather than red meat. Replace butter with margarine. Cut down to three eggs a week.
★ Boiling food washes out more vitamins than steaming food, which also preserves the flavour. Do not overcook food.

★ Avoid frying food. Grill, steam or bake instead.
★ Increase your fibre intake by eating wholemeal bread, cereals and pasta and eating brown instead of white rice.
★ Try to replace sugary snacks with fruit or raw vegetables.
★ Cut down on tea, coffee and sweet drinks and replace with herb teas and fruit juices.
★ Flavour food with herbs and spices instead of salt.

Food and your body

You use the food you eat for energy and to help you grow and to keep your body working properly. Below you can read how this happens.

On the opposite page you can read about weight-reducing diets, why you might feel you should lose weight and whether it is really necessary.

What happens to your food?

When you eat food it gets mashed up by your teeth and stomach into a pulp. Juices from your digestive system work on this pulp, breaking it down into tiny particles called molecules. These are absorbed into your blood and taken to different parts of your body.

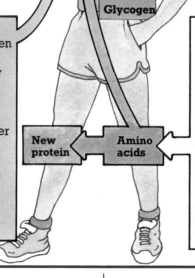

Energy

Glucose

Fatty acids and glycerol

Fat

Glycogen

New protein

Amino acids

Fats contain twice as much energy* as carbohydrates, weight for weight. During digestion, fats are broken down into fatty acids or glycerol. During prolonged exercise, these are converted to energy. Otherwise they are stored in fat cells under your skin and round your organs.

Carbohydrates are broken down by the body into glucose. When your body breaks this down further, energy is released. If you do not need it right away, glucose is stored in the liver or muscles as glycogen.

Extra carbohydrate is converted to fat. Exercise increases the storage capacity of glycogen, so you store less fat.

Proteins are broken down into molecules called amino acids. These are carried in the blood to all your body cells and rearranged into new proteins to form muscles, hair, skin, blood cells and so on. If you need a lot of energy for a long time or are starving, amino acids can be converted to glucose to provide energy.

Metabolic rates

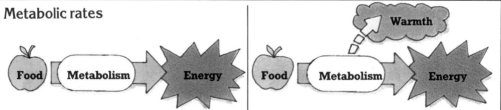

Food — **Metabolism** → **Energy**

Warmth

Food — **Metabolism** → **Energy**

The rate at which chemical processes, such as the digestion and absorption of food, take place in your body is known as your metabolic rate. Different people have slightly different metabolic rates. If you have a faster rate, you may be able to eat a lot without gaining fat because you use the calories quickly. If you have a slower metabolic rate, you may burn up food more slowly and gain fat easily.

Some people may have low metabolic rates and still not get fat. This is because after a meal certain special body cells burn up the excess energy, leaving little to be stored as fat. This generates heat, which is why you might feel warm after eating.

*Energy from food is measured in calories.

Losing weight

People come in all shapes and sizes.

There is a lot of unreasonable pressure nowadays, especially on girls and women, to conform to a certain shape. This may make people worry about their weight.

People weigh different amounts because they have different builds. A short, stocky person may weigh more than a tall, skinny person. Men tend to weigh more than women because they have more muscle on their bodies, which is a heavy tissue.

You do not need to lose weight unless you are storing so much extra fat on your body that it might strain your heart and be bad for you. If you are anxious about this, ask your doctor whether you should go on a controlled diet.

Fat-reducing diets

It is important that you do not go short of nutrients when you are growing. You will feel tired and your body may not be able to develop properly.

Diets where you eat only certain types of food, such as nothing but fruit, may leave you short of nutrients.

If your doctor agrees that you would be healthier if you got rid of some extra fat, he or she will probably give you a diet sheet. A sensible diet gives you all the nutrients you need.

Crash diets

BAD DIET
Starve yourself

GOOD DIET
Cut down on sugar, fat, salt, additives.
Increase fibre.
Eat fresh food.
Vary what you eat.

Severely cutting back on the amount you eat (going on a crash diet) can be dangerous. You are likely to go short of essential nutrients. You may appear to lose a lot of weight to start with but this is mainly water. You may burn up less energy because your muscles may shrink.

Changing your eating habits in the long term by cutting down on fat and sugar and increasing fibre intake is a far more effective way to lose fat than by going on a crash diet.

Exercise and losing weight

Healthy food + exercise = less fat stored on your body.

An effective way to lose fat is to combine healthy eating with taking exercise. This is because you burn up a lot of calories during prolonged exercise and your metabolic rate may be raised by 25% for between 15 hours and two days afterwards.

If you exercise regularly, your metabolic rate will be permanently increased.

When you start exercising regularly, you may find you put on weight. Although you are losing fat, you are building muscle which is heavy. Your general state of health will improve, though, and your body will be firmer.

Muscle is heavier than fat and you can do more with it.

27

All about skin

Your skin forms a barrier which keeps your body waterproof and prevents infections entering it. You can read about its other functions below. The opposite page shows how to deal with skin problems such as spots, over-greasy or dry skin.

Hair

Fat layer

Epidermis

Dermis

How your skin works

Your skin consists of two main layers: the outer layer, or epidermis, and the inner layer, or dermis. The cells at the base of the epidermis are constantly dividing. As cells are pushed out towards the surface, they die. The outside layer of dead cells is constantly being worn away and replaced with new cells from underneath.

Inner epidermis replacing top layer.

Top skin layer being worn away.

Sebaceous glands produce an oily substance called sebum. This lubricates your hair and skin and stops them drying out and cracking. It helps to keep your body waterproof, preventing germs from getting inside. If the glands produce too much sebum, your skin gets greasy.

Follicle (pit containing living root of hair).

Sebaceous gland

Sebum

Pores (openings in your skin leading from a sebaceous or sweat gland).

Sweat is produced by sweat glands in your dermis and comes out through pores. Sweat helps to cool you down when it evaporates off your skin. It contains dissolved waste matter.

Sweat gland

Sweat

When you are hot, your blood is pumped to the capillaries near the skin surface, so it can be cooled by being near the air. This is why you flush red when hot.

Blood vessels (capillaries) in hot weather.

When you are cold, these capillaries are blocked off so that less blood can reach them and less heat is lost. This is why you go pale when you are cold.

Capillaries in cold weather.

Nerve endings in your dermis sense pain, pressure, irritation, temperature and so on. They send the information along nerves to your brain.

Message to brain.

Nerve

Looking after your skin

Cleaning your skin rids it of dirt, make-up and the old, outer layers of dead skin which can block up pores and cause spots and infection.

 Soap and water are as good as cleansing lotions for cleaning skin. However, if your skin is dry and feels tight after washing with soap and water, use a cream cleanser instead. Massage your skin afterwards with moisturizer.

Eye make-up remover pads or lotions do not sting your eyes.

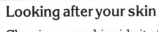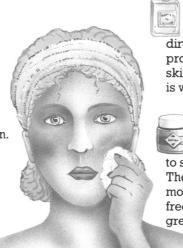

Astringent lotions may help to dissolve grease and remove dirt and they leave a protective barrier on your skin. A good natural one is witch hazel.

Moisturizers put a film on your skin's surface that helps to seal in its moisture. They do not add extra moisture. Use a grease-free moisturizer on greasy skin.

Improving your skin

Here are some hints on how to deal with different skin problems.

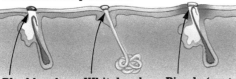

Blackhead (plug of dead cells and sebum in the pore). **Whitehead (tiny spot containing hardened sebum).** **Pimple (spot which has become infected and inflamed).**

Blackheads are caused by too many dead skin cells and too much sebum being produced. The cells go black on contact with oxygen in the air. Whiteheads are caused by blockages in the sebaceous or sweat glands. Pimples occur when a blockage to the pore of a sebaceous gland causes it to burst. The surrounding tissues become infected.

Blackhead remover —

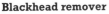

Fiddling with spots can introduce dirt and lead to infection. It is best to leave them alone. If you must, you can squeeze uninflamed blackheads and whiteheads with a blackhead remover, which you can buy. Sterilize it with an antiseptic and wash your hands first.

Oily skin

Oily skins look shiny and the pores may be visible. They may also be spottier than dry skins and attract more dirt.

Oily skins are caused by too much sebum. Use soap or a non-greasy liquid cleanser. Avoid rubbing the skin too vigorously as this may stimulate the sebaceous glands. Remove excess oil with an astringent lotion.

Acne

The changes that your body undergoes during adolescence often cause oily skin, which may develop into acne (dense areas of pimples). If you have acne, wash your face gently with mild soap to remove grease. Gels and lotions which peel off the top layer of the skin may help to unblock blackheads and pimples.

If your acne is bad your doctor may be able to help by prescribing creams or antibiotics, or by referring you to a skin specialist (dermatologist).

Dry skin

Dry skin feels tight and may look flaky. It becomes easily chapped and rough in cold or windy weather. It occurs when not enough sebum is produced, so that too much moisture is lost from the skin. Use a cream cleanser and moisturize the face and throat regularly.

Healthy hair

Because your hair cannot feel pain, it is easy to damage it by mistake. If you want to look after your hair properly, you may find it useful to understand its structure. You can read about this below and about why your hair is the colour and texture that it is.

The opposite page tells you what you can do about different hair problems and why they occur.

Your hair's structure

Each strand of hair has three layers. The outer layer, or cuticle, is made up of lots of scales, like a fish's skin. If the scales are smooth your hair looks glossy. If they are rough and damaged your hair looks dull.

The innermost layer is mostly spongy tissue.

Oily sebum from the sebaceous glands makes your hair glossy and supple and affects how greasy or dry it is.

Scalp

The shape of the pit, or follicle, that each hair grows from determines how curly or straight each one will be.

The middle layer, or cortex, consists of strong, elastic cells. They contain a substance called melanin which colours your hair. If you look at a handful of your hair you will see that it is made up of lots of different coloured hairs.

Each hair is attached to a muscle. These can contract and make your hairs stand on end, trapping warmth between hairs when you are cold.

Muscle

Follicle

Sweat gland

Washing your hair

Washing removes dirt, grease and dead cells from your scalp. Use a mild shampoo, such as baby shampoo, as the scalp can be irritated by strong ones. Some shampoos state how acidic or alkaline they are. This is measured as a pH value. pH1 is very acidic. pH14 is very alkaline. pH5 is about right for a shampoo as it is about the same level of acidity as your scalp.

Conditioning

Dry or damaged hair cuticle.

After conditioning.

Conditioners coat the hair shaft and smooth down the cuticle. This makes it easier to comb out tangles. They help to prevent dry hair and to increase gloss. Apply the conditioner to your hair, not to your scalp.

Drying your hair

The best way to dry hair is to let it dry naturally. Pat your hair gently, then wrap it in a towel for several minutes before combing carefully. Hair dryers can damage hair if they are too hot or held closer than six inches away.

Brushing and combing

Wide-spaced teeth

Round ends

Wide spaces between bristles.

Use a flexible, plastic comb with widely-spaced teeth with round ends. Start at the ends of your hair and work your way towards the roots, to avoid tearing hair. Use brushes with wide spaces between the bristles and keep them clean.

Brush your hair gently. Too much brushing can aggravate oily scalps.

Dandruff

This is a build-up of dead skin cells stuck together with sebum on the scalp. It is not an infection and does not respond to the antiseptic in medicated shampoos.

If you have dandruff, try washing your hair frequently and very gently with a mild shampoo. Anti-dandruff shampoos may irritate the scalp. Consult your doctor if your dandruff is very bad.

Greasy hair

Many people have greasy hair during adolescence. Shampoo it as often as it needs, if necessary every day. Use a mild shampoo, as strong brands often stimulate sebaceous glands to produce more oil. If you have split ends, apply conditioner only to the tips of your hair.

Dry hair

If your hair feels dry and brittle, avoid washing it more than is necessary to keep it clean, as this will reduce the amount of sebum in your hair. Use a conditioner. Gentle brushing will spread sebum down the hairs and keep your hair glossy.

Split ends

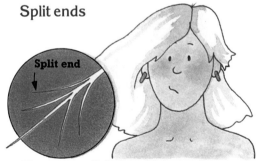

Split end

These are split hairs which may be caused by rough brushing and combing or using a hair dryer that is too hot. To prevent the split spreading up the hair, have your hair trimmed every two months.

Lice

These are little insects which lay eggs and stick them to the scalp. They are very hard to remove. The main symptom is itching. They are extremely contagious so you should treat them promptly. There are several different lotions on the market. You leave the lotion on to kill the eggs, then comb the eggs out.

Dyes, perms and bleaches

Dyeing, perming and bleaching all involve the use of chemicals which can weaken and damage hair.

Bonds between hair cells.   **Hair during perming.**   **Hair after perming.**

Perms work by breaking down the bonds between your hair cells and resetting them in a different shape.

Semi-permanent vegetable hair dyes are less harmful than permanent dyes.

You get dark, straight roots as bleached, permed hair grows out.

A vegetable dye washes out gradually so you do not get dark roots.

Hair care hints

★ If you want to put your hair up, use covered elastic bands, not rubber bands which will tear the cuticle.

★ Eat a healthy diet, containing plenty of vitamins and minerals.

★ Avoid overexposure to the sun, as it may damage your hair.

★ Avoid hairstyles that pull the hair tightly, such as tight ponytails or plaits, as they may tear your hair out.

Healthy teeth

Teeth seem to be tough and hard but if you neglect them they are easily damaged. Below is a diagram of how a tooth is constructed, followed by some of the problems you may get with your teeth and gums. Opposite you can read about how to look after them to keep them strong.

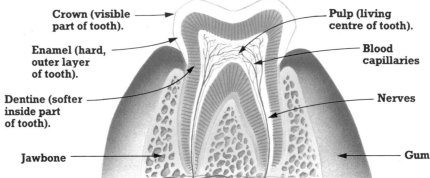

Crown (visible part of tooth).

Pulp (living centre of tooth).

Enamel (hard, outer layer of tooth).

Blood capillaries

Dentine (softer inside part of tooth).

Nerves

Jawbone

Gum

Toothache

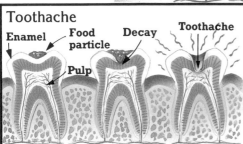

Enamel — Food particle — Decay — Toothache

Pulp

Your mouth contains bacteria which feed on food particles. As they feed, they produce acid which attacks the tooth enamel. A sticky white mixture of bacteria, food and acid, called plaque, builds up on your teeth. As the enamel gets eaten away, your teeth become sensitive to cold, heat and sweetness. If the decay carries on it may reach the inner pulp. If it hits a nerve you get toothache.

Cutting down on sweet foods and brushing your teeth after meals to remove plaque and food helps prevent decay.

Bad breath

Bad breath, or halitosis, may be caused by tooth decay, rotting food stuck between your teeth, infected gums, smoking, alcohol, bad colds or tonsillitis. There may be no obvious reason. A doctor or dentist can help you track down the cause.

A good natural way to help bad breath is to eat raw green vegetables such as parsley or lettuce.

Gum disease

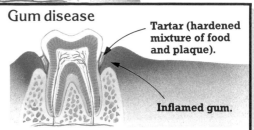

Tartar (hardened mixture of food and plaque).

Inflamed gum.

Plaque which is allowed to build up at the base of your teeth can cause gum disease. It forms a hard deposit, called tartar, which irritates the gums. Diseased gums may feel sore and bleed when you brush them. In serious cases, a tooth may loosen and fall out. Careful brushing and regular dental check-ups help to avoid this.

Crooked teeth

Some people have sticking out teeth, gaps between their teeth, or teeth growing at odd angles making it difficult to bite. Your dentist can straighten them using a light plastic device called a brace. Thin wires from this, attached to tiny springs, are looped round your teeth. Over a period of time, your dentist gradually tightens these wires to pull your teeth back into line.

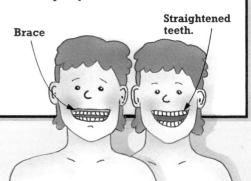

Brace

Straightened teeth.

Cleaning your teeth

You need to clean your teeth at least twice a day to rid them of plaque and food particles. Try to clean them after eating sweet things, too.

Brush biting surfaces and the base of your teeth next to the gums with small circular movements. Push the bristles into areas where plaque may collect. Do not brush your teeth vigorously backwards and forwards. This may damage gums and wear troughs in the teeth.

Use toothpicks to remove pieces of food stuck between your teeth.

You can clean between your teeth using a special thread called dental floss. You pull it gently up and down between your teeth to rub away the plaque.

Plaque is difficult to see. You can buy solutions or tablets called plaque disclosers. These go bright pink on contact with plaque to show where it is.

Brush upwards on the bottom teeth and downwards on the top teeth, both inside and out, to remove plaque from between them.

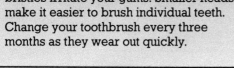

Use a soft toothbrush, as hard, spiky bristles irritate your gums. Smaller heads make it easier to brush individual teeth. Change your toothbrush every three months as they wear out quickly.

Many toothpastes contain a substance called fluoride. This helps to harden the enamel and makes it less vulnerable to acid. Many countries have fluoride in their water supplies.

Going to the dentist

Enamel

Fillings can be matched to the colour of your tooth.

Tartar and plaque.

Dirty tooth

The dentist scrapes off tartar which a toothbrush cannot remove.

Tooth after scraping and polishing.

You should have your teeth checked by a dentist at least twice a year so that problems can be treated before they get serious.

Dentists scrape tartar and plaque off your teeth and polish them. They remove decay by drilling away the bad area and filling the hole with a substance that hardens. This prevents the decay spreading. They can put new tops, or crowns, on badly damaged teeth, matching them to the others.

33

Taking care of your eyes

Your eyes work by picking up light rays reflected by objects around you. Cells lining the back of your eyes are sensitive to these rays and send the information they receive to your brain. On these two pages, you can find out more about this and how to keep your eyes healthy and shining.

How your eyes work

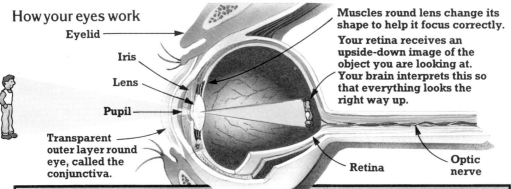

Eyelid

Iris

Lens

Pupil

Transparent outer layer round eye, called the conjunctiva.

Muscles round lens change its shape to help it focus correctly.

Your retina receives an upside-down image of the object you are looking at. Your brain interprets this so that everything looks the right way up.

Retina

Optic nerve

Light rays enter your eyeball through the pupil. This is the black hole in the centre of your eye.	The coloured iris round the pupil alters the size of the pupil to control the amount of light entering the eye.	The light rays are focussed by a lens so that they fall on to the retina which lines the back of the eye.	The retina contains cells which are sensitive to light and colour. The optic nerve sends messages from the retina to the brain.

Poor eyesight

Poor eyesight is usually caused by light rays not being focussed correctly on the retina. Things look blurred. This happens when the eyeball gets out of shape. It can be corrected by wearing glasses or contact lenses which bend the rays before they enter your eyes so they focus correctly on your retina (see below).

Testing your eyesight

If you cannot read a telephone directory with each eye at 49cm (19ins) or a car number plate at 23m (25yds), you should have your eyes checked as you may need glasses.

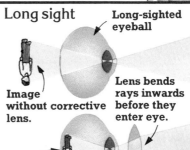

Short sight

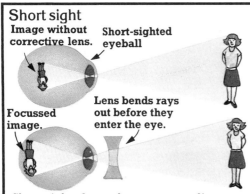

Image without corrective lens.

Short-sighted eyeball

Focussed image.

Lens bends rays out before they enter the eye.

Short-sighted people cannot see distant objects clearly. The eyeball is too long and distant images are focussed before they reach the retina.

Long sight

Long-sighted eyeball

Image without corrective lens.

Lens bends rays inwards before they enter eye.

Focussed image.

Long-sighted people find it difficult to see close objects clearly. The eyeball is too short and images reach the retina before being focussed.

Choosing glasses

There are lots of different styles of glasses available. Light ones are less likely to give you headaches and rub your skin than heavy ones. They need to fit snugly so they do not slide down your nose.

Some glasses have shaded lenses. Others have lenses that react to different levels of light. They go dark in the sun to protect your eyes.

Contact lenses

Contact lenses may be easier to wear than glasses if you are very active. They float on the surface of your eye in front of the pupil. Soft contact lenses are more expensive and more comfortable but they need replacing about every two years.

Hard lenses last longer, although you need to replace them if your eyesight changes.

Dirt in your eyes

Tear gland, or lachrymal gland, above outside corner of eye.

Tears drain across eye into lachrymal sac.

Your eyes clean themselves naturally by producing tear fluid. This is why they water if you get dust in them. You can stimulate more tears by blowing your nose. If you get something in your eye you may be able to remove it by gently pulling the upper lid over the lower lid.

Never stick anything in your eye as you may damage it. If you cannot remove something from your eye, go to your local hospital casualty department.

Tired eyes

Looking into the blackness of your cupped hands relaxes the irises and the muscles round the lenses of your eyes.

If you do too much close work, especially in dim light, you may strain your eyes. Your eye muscles ache and you may get a headache. You may not blink enough so your eyes feel dry and sore.

Blinking a few times washes your eyes with tears and helps relieve soreness. Focussing on a distant object and gently rolling your eyes helps to relieve aching muscles. Cupping your hands over open eyes for a few minutes helps to rest them.

Bloodshot eyes

Camomile

Camomile tea bag.

If you are tired or have been outside in windy weather, your eyes may look bloodshot. This is caused by a dilation of blood capillaries in the conjunctiva.

You can relieve bloodshot eyes by soaking two camomile tea bags in cold water and placing one bag on each eye. The cold water and the camomile have a soothing, anti-inflammatory effect.

Eye infections

Conjunctivitis   Blepharitis   Stye

If your eyes are sticky, red, watery or painful, you may have an infection and should see your doctor. Conjunctivitis is an infection of the conjunctiva.

If the hair follicles of your eyelashes are inflamed making the eye look red-rimmed, it is called blepharitis.

The base of an eyelash may become infected and swell to form a stye. Do not use ointments on styes. Gently pressing cotton wool soaked in warm water against the stye may soothe it.

Caring for hands and feet

Your hands and feet are complex arrangements of lots of little bones. They get a lot of use, so it is worth looking after them. If your hands are sore or your feet hurt, life can be very uncomfortable.

Looking after your hands

If you put your hands in water a lot and do not dry them properly, they may get sore and scaly. Tap water is a very weak solution of chemicals but it is stronger than the moisture in your skin. Moisture moves out through the epidermis in an attempt to dilute the tap water. The process of water moving through a barrier to dilute a solution on the other side is called osmosis.

Rubber glove

Sweat

Sweat gland

Epidermis

Tap water

Moisture from skin.

Epidermis

Wearing rubber gloves helps to protect your hands against water and detergents which dry out skin. If you wear gloves for longer than a few minutes, though, your hands will sweat a lot, which also dries them out. Hand cream helps prevent your hands from drying out or cracking in cold weather. You can also buy waterproof barrier creams to protect your hands when washing up and so on.

Nails

Like hair, nails are made up of dead cells growing from a living root, or matrix. This is underneath the cuticle at the base of the nail.

White spots on nails are caused by knocks to the matrix which damage new nail cells.

Keep cuticles supple by rubbing hand cream into them. Do not poke them with hard objects or you may hurt the matrix.

Nail

Cuticle

Matrix

Bruised-looking nails may be caused by ill health, anaemia or smoking.

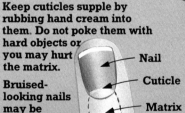

Biting your nails

Biting nails weakens them and dirt from under them ends up in your mouth. You can buy bitter solutions to brush on your nails to help you stop biting them.

Cutting your nails

Cut your nails in an oval shape, level with the ends of your fingers. You may find it easier to do this using nail clippers or curved nail scissors.

File away rough edges with an emery board. File in one direction as going backwards and forwards splits nails.

Remove dirt from under nails with the tip of an orange stick wrapped in cotton wool.

Looking after your feet

Your feet are made up of many bones, held in place by ligaments. It is easy to hurt your feet if you wear shoes which do not fit properly.

Buying shoes

Try shoes on and walk around before you buy them. Your feet swell up during the day and when it is hot, so take this into account when trying shoes on.

Shoes should fit snugly at your ankle so you do not have to bunch your toes up to keep them on.

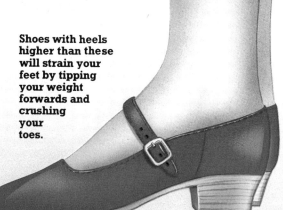

Shoes with heels higher than these will strain your feet by tipping your weight forwards and crushing your toes.

Shoes should be wide enough to let your toes lie naturally and not be squashed.

They should be about 1cm (1/3 in) longer than the foot to allow free movement.

Tired feet

Tired feet are often caused by ill-fitting shoes, high heels or non-stretch tights. Your ankles may swell if you are on your feet all day, especially in hot weather.

You can reduce swelling and rest your feet by lying down with your feet raised on cushions.

Flat feet

If the muscles forming the arch of your foot are weak, you may get flat feet. They may be strained by carrying your weight. These exercises should help:

1. With feet together, slowly rise up on tiptoes and down again. Repeat five times.

2. Put a pencil on the floor, place your toes over it and try to pick it up. Do this several times with each foot.

3. Walking barefoot is a good all-round exercise for feet.

Bunions

If you wear shoes that are too tight your big toe is bent sideways against your other toes. The joint may become inflamed and form a swelling called a bunion. If it becomes very painful this can be removed by surgery.

Athlete's Foot

If your skin is sore and peels in between your toes you may have an infection called Athlete's Foot. This is a fungus which grows on warm, damp feet. You can buy special creams or powders at a chemist to get rid of it.

Chilblains

In very cold weather, you may get painful, itchy patches on your toes, ankles, legs or hands. This is the result of blood vessels contracting excessively in the cold, cutting off the blood supply to parts of the tissue, which damages it. When you warm up, the damaged tissue hurts. Keep these parts warm with extra clothing. You can buy creams to help relieve chilblains.

Ingrown toenails

An ingrown toenail is a toenail that has curved over at the sides and grown into the flesh. This may happen naturally or it may be caused by tight shoes or socks. To prevent ingrown toenails, do not cut your nails too short or cut them away at the sides.

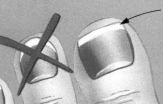

Cut toenails straight across. Do not try to shape them at the sides.

Looking after your back

Many people suffer from backache and related aches and pains. You can avoid some of these by taking care that you do not strain your back by standing and sitting or lifting and carrying things in the wrong way. Below you can see how your back works and how to avoid straining it.

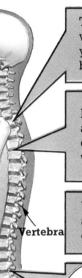

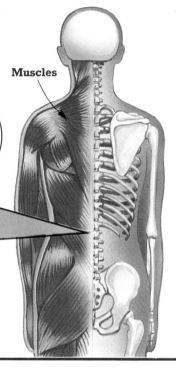

Muscles

The line of knobbly bones, called vertebrae, down the middle of your back is your spine. It forms an S-shaped column between your skull and hips.

In between your vertebrae are discs of gristle, or cartilage, with soft centres which absorb shock.

Disc

Vertebra

Your spine is held in position by muscles and ligaments. Some of these connect to other parts of your body.

Spinal cord

A column of nerves called the spinal cord runs through the vertebrae. It carries messages between your brain and lower body.

Using your back

Good posture means holding your body in a balanced way. This prevents you putting uneven pressure on your muscles and straining them.

Standing

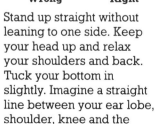

Wrong   **Right**

Stand up straight without leaning to one side. Keep your head up and relax your shoulders and back. Tuck your bottom in slightly. Imagine a straight line between your ear lobe, shoulder, knee and the front of your ankle.

Sitting

Wrong   **Right**

The best seat height for your back allows your feet to rest on the floor with your thighs parallel to the floor. This avoids straining your lower back. A firm back rest helps. Do not cross your legs as this uses your back unevenly.

Sleeping

Soft mattress

Firm mattress

On a soft mattress, some of your back muscles have to work harder than others to support your spine. You can put planks under your mattress to make it firmer. Use enough pillows so that your head is supported in line with your spine.

Back strains

It is easy to damage the muscles, ligaments or tendons surrounding the spine by moving or twisting in an awkward way. This kind of strain usually heals itself in time but can be painful. You can soothe it by keeping the muscles warm with hot water bottles or baths. Always see your doctor if it is very bad.

Disc trouble

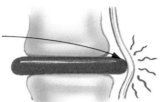

Slipped disc pressing against nerve.

If you continually hold your back in the wrong way and put pressure on it, you may cause one of your discs to slip out of position. This is called a slipped disc. If the damaged disc presses against a spinal nerve it can cause a lot of pain.

Slipped discs can be treated with rest, massage, heat treatment or one of the treatments described on the right. You can wear special supportive corsets. A board under your mattress will support your spine while you sleep.

Alexander Technique

The Alexander Technique is a way of improving posture. It is named after the doctor who invented it. He believed that bad posture causes all kinds of physical problems, including bad backs. The treatment involves massage, exercise and learning how to sit, stand and move properly.

Osteopathy and chiropractic

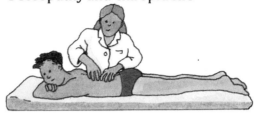

Osteopathy and chiropractic are ways of treating physical disorders by forms of massage and manipulation. The treatments are often used for back problems, though osteopaths and chiropractors believe that other illnesses can also be treated by working on the spine.

Exercise
Exercise such as yoga, swimming, walking and stretching all strengthen your back and help your posture.

Bending

Wrong   Right

Carrying

Hold single weights close in front of you.

Shifting heavier weights

When lifting things, bend your legs and keep your back as straight as possible. This is because your leg muscles are stronger than your back muscles. Kneel to do things such as cleaning the bath instead of bending over.

When carrying a weight such as a typewriter or a baby, hold it close in front of you. Rather than carrying one bag of shopping, carry two smaller ones, one in each hand. This prevents the spine from being pulled sideways.

The safest way to shift a heavy weight is to lean your back against it and push. When pushing things such as a lawn mower, put your whole body into it. Try to move heavy furniture by rocking it rather than lifting it.

Rest and relaxation

Rest and relaxation are just as important to your body as exercise and healthy eating. If you do not get enough of them you can make yourself ill. Your body is a bit like a battery. If it is not allowed to recharge itself through sleep and relaxation it may stop working properly.

Why you need sleep

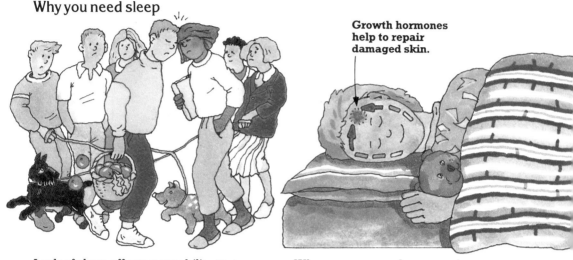

Growth hormones help to repair damaged skin.

Lack of sleep affects your ability to concentrate. When you dream, your brain may be clearing itself out and preparing itself for the next day's thinking.

During your teens, you need at least eight hours sleep a night. If you stay out late, try to go to bed early the next night. The effects of lack of sleep can build up over several days.

When you are awake you make many demands on your mind and body. Your body needs a period of rest to repair itself and prevent itself from getting worn out. During sleep, substances called hormones stimulate body tissues to grow and repair themselves.

Children need more sleep than adults because there is more growing to do.

Preparing for a better sleep

If you have trouble getting to sleep, or want a really good night's sleep, try the following things.

Leave a window slightly open but make sure you are warm enough.

Try reading a book to calm your mind.

Take some exercise during the evening. This will help your muscles relax.

Avoid tea, coffee, or food before bedtime. A hot, milky drink may help you relax, though.

What causes stress?

When you feel anger, fear or anxiety your body produces hormones such as adrenalin and noradrenalin to gear it up for action. They prepare your body for fighting or running away.

If you are continually anxious, your body goes through this reaction over and over again. This can cause stress. If you do not carry out the physical responses for which your body is prepared, the hormones build up. This leads to tension and tiredness.

Stress can lower your resistance to illness and lead to headaches, indigestion and sleeplessness. It may in time lead to more serious complaints such as asthma, stomach ulcers, high blood pressure and heart disease.

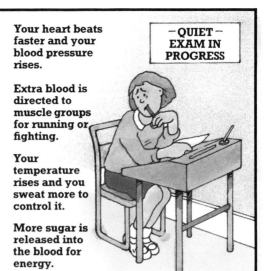

Your heart beats faster and your blood pressure rises.

Extra blood is directed to muscle groups for running or fighting.

Your temperature rises and you sweat more to control it.

More sugar is released into the blood for energy.

Your breathing becomes deeper and faster to take in more oxygen.

How to avoid stress

Try to work out the causes of your anxiety. Discuss it with someone and try to find a way of avoiding it or changing your attitude to it. Set aside part of each day for relaxation.

Relaxation

Lie on the floor or on your bed.	Tense your toes as tightly as you can, then slowly relax them.	Carry on slowly tensing and relaxing all the different muscle groups in your body, travelling up your legs and the rest of your body.

If you are anxious, your body may be tense even if you are not aware of it. This can be exhausting. The exercise above might help you to relax.

Deep breathing

If you are upset you may breathe in short sharp pants, using only the top half of your rib cage. To calm down, breathe deeply and slowly several times, making your chest rise and fall. Breathing like this can help you calm down before a stressful experience such as an interview.

Meditation

If your mind is buzzing with worries you may feel tired but be unable to relax. You can relax your mind by concentrating on something soothing. This is known as meditation. You can learn the techniques in special classes and it is also used in Yoga. Here is a meditation exercise. Keep at it for at least ten minutes.

Sit comfortably, close your eyes and try to relax. Breathe regularly. Think of a soothing scene, such as a peaceful lake and concentrate on it. Try to blot out other thoughts.

Massage

If you are under stress, your neck and shoulder muscles tend to tense up which may give you headaches. Massaging them will help you relax them. Here is a simple massage you can do with a friend.

1. Sit your friend down and stand behind him or her.

2. Place hands on shoulders, thumbs reaching down back.

3. Gently squeeze muscles and flesh without pinching.

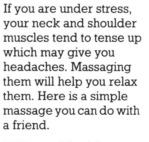

Smoking, alcohol and drugs

Advertisements may make you think that alcoholic drinks or cigarettes will make you feel good. Although they may be pleasant at first, they can be bad for you in the long term and they can become addictive (very difficult to give up). Here you can find out about the effects cigarettes and alcohol can have on your body and also about what other drugs, such as pot, do to you.

What smoking does to you

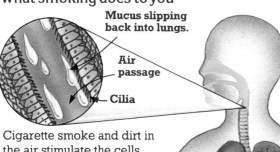

Mucus slipping back into lungs.

Air passage

Cilia

A smoker's lungs become blackened with tar.

Cigarette smoke and dirt in the air stimulate the cells lining your air passages to produce more mucus, or phlegm.

The mucus traps any dirt and it is pushed back up your air passages by little hairs, called cilia. By blowing your nose or spitting it out you keep your lungs clear.

When you inhale cigarette smoke, your cilia stop working. Mucus carrying waste substances, tar and nicotine slips back down into your lungs. Eventually the cilia stop working even when you are not smoking.

Lung cancer
Certain cells in your lungs fight bacteria by engulfing them. They also engulf tar from smoke. Chemicals in the tar can start lung cells changing into cancer cells which multiply, destroy the lungs and spread around the body to start new cancers.

Chronic bronchitis
Tar and mucus may damage the small air tubes and air sacs in your lungs. This can lead to dangerous diseases such as chronic bronchitis. This makes you pant when taking even gentle exercise.

Heart disease
Carbon dioxide and other gases in cigarette smoke increase your pulse rate and blood pressure. This may cause fatty deposits to build up in your arteries, leading to severe heart disease.

Reasons not to smoke

Here are some reasons why you should not start smoking.

★ Most people do not smoke because they do not want to risk their lives. They also prefer not to have to put up with other people's smoke.

★ Cigarette smoke makes your clothes, hair and breath stink.

★ It is unpleasant for non-smokers to kiss or come into close contact with smokers.

If you decide to stop smoking, here are some things which might help.

★ Take up a new sport or fitness activity. The fitter you become, the less you will want to damage your lungs with cigarettes.

★ For a couple of months, put the money you would otherwise spend on cigarettes in a jar. Then buy yourself a treat with it at the end.

★ Tell your friends you have given up and ask them not to offer you cigarettes.

What does alcohol do to you?

Alcohol is in drinks such as beer, wine and spirits. A couple of drinks cannot harm you but alcohol can easily become addictive. Below you can read about what happens to alcohol in your body.

Alcohol taken to brain while waiting to enter liver.

Your liver can only absorb 28gm (1/3 oz) of alcohol per hour.

This equals:
1/3 glass of beer.
or
1/9 bottle of wine.
or
7/10 measure of spirits.

Alcohol is a mild poison. If you drink more than a small amount it is pumped round your body in your blood while it waits to be absorbed and neutralized by your liver.

When it reaches your brain, it affects your speech, actions, senses and judgement. This is why it is very dangerous to drive if you have been drinking. Too much alcohol causes headaches, sickness and thirst the next day. This is called a hangover.

Why drinking can be dangerous

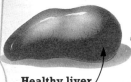

Healthy liver   **Liver after years of heavy drinking.**

If you drink heavily, your liver has to continually overwork to digest the alcohol and make you sober. This may lead to liver damage, including fatal diseases such as cirrhosis of the liver.

Part of stomach eaten away by digestive juices.

Heavy drinking and an inadequate diet tend to inflame parts of your stomach and upper intestine. These then get eaten away by digestive juices, creating painful sores called peptic ulcers.

Too much alcohol can also damage your brain and weaken your heart muscles.

Being addicted to alcohol is a disease known as alcoholism. It can be cured and you should seek help from your doctor if you or anyone you know is an addict.

How other drugs affect you

There are a number of other drugs which you may be tempted to try. People may tell you stories about the wonderful feelings that they give you. However they cause your body enormous harm; thousands of people die from drug abuse every year. Below you can find out about some of the most common drugs.

Drug and description	Danger
Marijuana. Known as pot or hash. Usually smoked.	Similar dangers to tobacco, as it irritates your lungs. Can create malformed sperm and harm unborn babies.
Spirit-based glue. Usually sniffed.	Contains complex chemicals which can destroy your nasal tissue and damage your lungs.
Cocaine. Fine white powder derived from cocoa shrub. Usually sniffed.	This drug can damage your lungs for life. Highly addictive and very expensive.
LSD. Usually taken in white pills.	LSD puts you in a strange, sometimes terrifying world. This is called a "trip". It can cause permanent brain damage.
Heroin. Greyish-brown powder from the juice of the poppy flower, or artificially made.	One of the most addictive and poisonous of all drugs. Your body quickly gets used to a high level and needs more. Heroin addicts suffer pain and become desperate if they cannot get enough.
Tranquillizers, stimulants and sleeping pills.	Some people find these drugs addictive if they take them for too long.

Growing up

Between the ages of about 10 and 18 you go through many physical and emotional changes. This time, called puberty, is the stage between being a child and being an adult.

During puberty, your body starts to produce more hormones which stimulate your body to change. The pictures show some of these changes and how to deal with them.

What happens to boys?

Your voice box, or larynx, grows bigger, making your voice break. While this is happening, your voice might sound husky or alternate between being squeaky and deep.

You grow hair on your face and eventually need to start shaving. You can probably get rid of hair fastest using an electric razor. However, foam, warm water and a non-electric razor may give you a closer shave.

You grow hair and new sweat glands under your arms and around your penis. Sweat starts to smell sour after a few hours. You may get used to the smell yourself but others will notice it. Make sure you wash these areas once a day. You can use a deodorant under your arms as well to prevent the smell of stale sweat.

Your chest and shoulders get broader as you develop a bigger heart and lungs. These changes happen slowly.

Some boys grow hair on their chests.

Over the years you develop more muscle. The exercises and activities shown earlier in the book, especially on pages 8-9, 14-15 and 20-21 will help you build muscle.

Your penis and testes get bigger. The left testis usually hangs down slightly lower than the right one.
    The testes start to produce sperm (male sex cells) and the male sex hormone, which is called testosterone. This hormone is responsible for many of the other changes that take place in your body during puberty.

Different parts of your body grow at different rates. Your limbs might grow very fast and you might get taller before you get broader. You may feel gangly and awkward for a while.

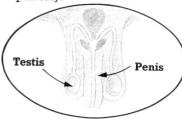

Testis   Penis

What happens to girls?

Hair grows under your arms and around your vagina. You can shave underarm hair if you like but many women do not.

More sweat glands develop in these areas so wash them once a day. You can wear a deodorant under your arms. (See the advice given for boys on the previous page.)

Inside your body, parts of you develop to enable you to have children. Your ovaries start to produce an egg each month. Unless it is fertilized by a sperm and you get pregnant, your body discharges the egg along with the womb's lining of blood. This is called your period and lasts a few days.

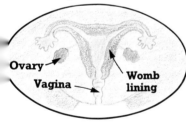

Ovary
Vagina
Womb lining

You can use a tampon or a sanitary towel to absorb your period blood. You need to change them two or three times a day. You can go swimming or do any exercise wearing a tampon. It cannot slip. Sanitary towels are absorbent pads which you wear between your legs.

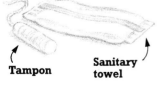

Tampon
Sanitary towel

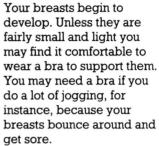

Your breasts begin to develop. Unless they are fairly small and light you may find it comfortable to wear a bra to support them. You may need a bra if you do a lot of jogging, for instance, because your breasts bounce around and get sore.

Everyone is a different shape so try several bras and find one that suits you before you buy one.

You cannot alter your breast size by exercising as breasts contain no muscles. However, exercise such as swimming can strengthen surrounding muscles and help them support your breasts.

Your hips get wider so that they will be broad enough to carry a baby and give birth.

Some women get pains in the lower stomach and back before or during a period. You can buy painkillers for this. It is caused by the womb contracting to push out the blood. Gentle activity may help, such as swimming or walking.

You may also feel particularly moody, depressed or tearful before a period. Be patient with yourself and the moods will pass. If any of these problems gets really bad, see a doctor.

45

Checking your fitness progress

Fitness quiz

Answer this quiz, then add up your scores from the list on the right. Your total tells you which fitness category you are in.

1. **How often do you eat fresh fruit?**
    a. two or three times a week
    b. every day
    c. never
2. **To pick up a heavy load, do you:**
    a. bend over from the waist, reach down and pick up the weight?
    b. bend your knees, take the weight, then rise?
    c. ask someone stronger to help you?
3. **How many of the following exercises do you do once a week or more?**
    brisk walking   swimming
    jogging   skipping
    bicycle riding   other exercise
4. **How many eggs do you eat in a week?**
    a. more than 6
    b. between 3 and 6
    c. 2 or less
5. **Is your pulse within the target training zone (see pages 8-9)?**
    a. yes   b. no
6. **How many chocolate bars or packets of sweets do you eat in a week?**
    a. 1 or 2
    b. more than 5
    c. 3 or 4
7. **How many press-ups can you easily do?**
    a. less than 5
    b. between 5 and 10
    c. over 10
8. **Can you touch your toes?**
    a. yes   b. no
9. **Do you smoke?**
    a. yes   b. no
10. **What effect does running up a flight of stairs have on you?**
    a. it makes you pant slightly
    b. you are hardly out of breath
    c. you breathe hard for several minutes
11. **When did you last go to the dentist?**
    a. less than 6 months ago
    b. between 6 months and a year ago
    c. over a year ago
12. **Do you take sugar in hot drinks?**
    a. yes   b. no

Scores

1. a.1   b.2   c.0
2. a.0   b.2   c.1
3. For each exercise you do once a week, score 1. For each one you do more than once, score 2.
4. a.0   b.1   c.2
5. a.1   b.0
6. a.2   b.0   c.1
7. a.0   b.1   c.2
8. a.1   b.0
9. a.0   b.1
10. a.1   b.2   c.0
11. a.2   b.1   c.0
12. a.0   b.1

Fitness categories:

0-6 You are either very unfit, very young or very old. Start improving your fitness gradually. Try and improve your diet and very slowly build up the amount of exercise you do.

7-14 Your general fitness level is still low. To make progress, take more gentle exercise and push yourself slowly to increase the amount you can manage.

15-22 You are quite fit but could still improve. Stick to a healthy diet and try to increase your performance at exercise.

23-20 You are probably very fit. You can progress by building up exercise levels and concentrating on weaknesses.

Measuring your progress

If you are trying to improve your fitness, it helps to keep a record of your progress. If you particularly want to develop your strength, try counting how many press-ups or other strengthening exercises (see pages 14-15) you can manage each week.

Measuring how your suppleness improves is also quite easy. Stand in front of a mirror and do some of the suppleness exercises on pages 18-19. See how much further you can bend each week.

Measure your stamina progress by copying the chart opposite and marking your pulse rate before and after stamina activities. If you are unfit, your pulse rate after exercise will gradually rise into the target training zone (page 9). As you get fitter you will be able to do more for less effort. Your pulse rate after exercise may drop, and you may have to do more to keep it in the target training zone. The pulse rates shown here are only examples.

Getting fit

Below you can find out about the sports and activities you can do to improve your stamina, strength and suppleness. Many sports appear under more than one heading: these are good for improving fitness in general. If, however, you are interested in developing one aspect of fitness, (say, your strength), you should concentrate on a selection of the sports listed under that heading. Sports which are especially good for developing a particular aspect of fitness are shown in bold type.

STAMINA

badminton
basketball
boxing
cycling
dancing
football (rugby and soccer)
gymnastics
brisk walking
hockey
jogging
netball
rowing
running
skating (roller and ice)
skiing (cross-country)
skipping
squash
swimming
tennis
wind-surfing

STRENGTH

badminton
boxing
canoeing
fencing
football (rugby and soccer)
gymnastics
hockey
horse-riding
judo
netball
rowing
running
sailing
skating (roller and ice)
skiing (cross-country)
squash
swimming
tennis
weight-training
wind-surfing

SUPPLENESS

badminton
dancing
fencing
football (rugby and soccer)
cricket
gymnastics
judo
netball
rock-climbing
sailing
skating (roller and ice)
skiing (cross-country)
squash
swimming
table-tennis
tennis
yoga

The pulse rates shown below might be for a young person who is not very fit.

	Activity	Time spent exercising	Pulse before activity	Pulse after activity
Example ▶	SWIMMING DANCING BADMINTON	15 MINUTES 1½ HOURS 1 HOUR	72 68 75	125 119 105
Week 1				
Week 2				
Week 3				
Week 4				
Week 5				
Week 6				

Index

acne, 29
adrenalin, 41
aerobic,
    exercise, 7, 8-9, 12
    system, 7
alcohol, 3, 32, 42, 43
Alexander Technique, 39
anaerobic respiration, 12
arteries, 6, 7, 25, 42
arthritis, 3, 25
asthma, 8, 23
Athlete's Foot, 37
athletics, 20
ATP, 12
back, 13, 38-39
backache, 3, 38
bad breath, see halitosis
badminton, 20
ballet, 19
biceps, 12, 15
blackhead, 29
blepharitis, 35
blood, 5, 6, 7, 8, 9, 12, 23,
    26, 45
    high blood pressure, 7, 8,
    14, 23, 25, 41, 42
bones, 2, 12, 16, 36, 37, 38
brain, 12, 28, 34, 43
breasts, 45
breathing, 10, 41
caffeine, 25
calories, 26
cancer, 3, 42
canoeing, 14
carbohydrate, 24, 25
carrying loads, 17, 39
cartilage, 16, 38
chest, 4, 5, 6, 44
chilblains, 37
chiropractic, 39
cholesterol, 25
cocaine, 43
conjunctivitis, 35
constipation, 24
contact lenses, 34, 35
coughs, 5
cramp, 13
cuticle,
    hair, 30
    nail, 36
cycling, 8
dancing, 19
dandruff, 31
dermatologist, 29
dermis, 28
diabetes, 8, 23
diet, 13, 24, 25, 26, 27, 31, 40
    43
digestion, 3, 23, 24, 26, 43
disc, slipped, 39
drugs, 3, 42, 43
energy, 2, 3, 4, 8, 12, 24,
    25, 26
epidermis, 28, 36
exercise, 2, 5, 6-11, 13, 14-15,
    17, 18-19, 20-21, 22, 23,
    40, 44, 45

eyes, 34-35
eyesight, poor, 34
fat, 4, 24, 25, 26, 27
feet, 5, 36, 37
fibre, 24, 25, 27
fluoride, 33
food, 3, 4, 6, 7, 23, 24-25,
    26-27, 32, 33
glands,
    lachrymal (tear), 35
    sebaceous, 28, 29
    sweat, 28, 29, 36, 44, 45
glasses, 34, 35
glue, 43
growing up, 3, 44-45
gums, 32, 33
gymnastics, 19
hair, 3, 30-31, 44, 45
halitosis, 32
hands, 5, 36
hangover, 43
heart, 4, 5, 6, 7, 8, 9, 27, 44
    disease, 3, 5, 7, 25, 41, 42
heroin, 43
hormones, 40, 41, 44
ice skating, 19
ingrown toenails, 37
injuries, 17, 22-23
isometric exercise, 14
jogging, 8, 10-11, 45
joints, 4, 5, 8, 16, 17, 22, 23
lice, 31
ligaments, 16, 17, 37, 38, 39
liver, cirrhosis of, 43
LSD, 43
lungs, 6, 7, 8, 42, 43, 44
marijuana, 43
massage, 13, 39, 41
meditation, 41
melanin, 30
metabolic rate, 4, 26, 27
metabolism, 4
minerals, 24, 25, 31
mucus, 42
muscles, 2, 4, 6, 7, 9, 10,
    12-13, 16, 17, 18, 22, 23,
    26, 27, 30, 34, 35, 38, 39
    40, 41, 44, 45
    strengthening, 8, 14-15
nails, 36, 37
nerves, 28, 32, 34, 39
nicotine, 42
noradrenalin, 41
nutrients, 27
osteopathy, 39
ovaries, 45
over-exercising, 5, 9, 13, 17,
    22
oxygen, 4, 5, 6, 7, 12, 29
penis, 44
period, 45
phlegm, 42
pimple, 29
plaque, 32, 33
pores, 28, 29
posture, 3, 13, 17, 38-39
pot belly, 13

protein, 24, 26
puberty, 44
pulse,
    how to take your, 7
    rate, 7, 9
relaxation, 3, 8, 17, 40-41
riding, 14
rowing, 14
salt, 25
sanitary towel, 45
sebum, 28, 29, 30, 31
shaving, 44
shoes, ill-fitting, 37
skiing, cross-country, 14
skin, 3, 26, 28-29, 31
skipping, 8
sleep, 3, 38, 40, 41
sleeping pills, 43
smoking, 3, 7, 32, 42
sodium nitrate, 25
sperm, 43, 44, 45
spine, 13, 38, 39
sports, 2, 20, 21, 22
spots, 25, 28, 29
sprains, 17, 23
squash, 20
stamina, 2, 8-9, 12, 20, 21,
    22, 47
stiffness, 8, 17
strains, 18, 22, 23, 39
strength, 2, 8, 12, 14-15, 20,
    21, 47
stress, 3, 7, 41
stye, 35
suppleness, 2, 5, 8, 16-17,
    18-19, 21, 22, 47
sweat, 28, 36, 44
swimming, 8, 45
synovial fluid, 16
tampon, 45
tar, 42
tartar, 32, 33
tartrazine, 25
teeth, 25, 32-33
tendon, 12, 16, 22, 39
tennis, 20
tension, 3, 41
testis, 44
testosterone, 44
tiredness, 22, 35, 41
trainers, 9, 10, 11, 22
training, 8-9, 10-11, 20-21
tranquillizers, 43
triceps, 12, 15
vagina, 45
vertebrae, 38
vitamins, 24, 25, 31
voice, breaking, 44
walking, 8, 45
warming up, 8, 10, 13, 15, 17,
    22
water, 24
weight, losing, 27
weights, 12, 14-15
whitehead, 29
womb, 45
yoga, 19, 41

First published in 1985 by Usborne Publishing Ltd., Usborne House, 83-85 Saffron Hill, London EC1N 8RT.

© Usborne Publishing 1991, 1985

The name Usborne and the device 🐝 are Trade Marks of Usborne Publishing Ltd.

Printed in Belgium